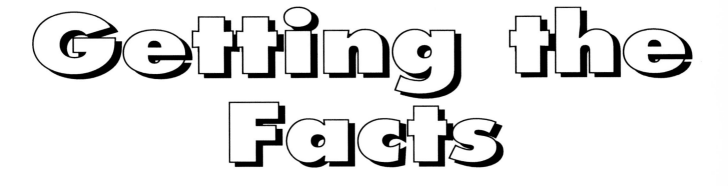

© Aladdin Books Ltd 1998
Produced by
Aladdin Books Ltd
28 Percy Street
London W1P OLD

First published in the United States
in 1998 by
Copper Beech Books,
an imprint of
The Millbrook Press
2 Old New Milford Road
Brookfield, Connecticut 06804

Project Editor: Sally Hewitt
Editor: Liz White
Design: David West Children's Book Design
Designer: Simon Morse
Photography: Roger Vlitos
Illustrator: Tony Kenyon

Printed in Belgium
5 4 3 2 1

CIP data is on file at the Library of Congress.
ISBN 0-7613-0816-4 (lib. bdg.)
ISBN 0-7613-0735-4 (trade pbk.)

MATH *for fun*

Getting the Facts

Andrew King

COPPER BEECH BOOKS
BROOKFIELD, CONNECTICUT

CONTENTS

INTRODUCTION

Collecting information, making sense of it, and using it are skills that people doing all kinds of different jobs have to do every day. Being able to think logically and make strategies can help you to do many things better, from winning games to solving tricky problems.

Try the exciting activities, practical projects, and fun games in this book, and you can learn to think logically, work out the chances, make and use graphs, and solve problems.

● Follow the STEP-BY-STEP INSTRUCTIONS to help you with the activities.

● Use the HELPFUL HINTS for clues about the experiments and games.

● Look at MORE IDEAS for information about other projects.

 Yellow squares mean this is an easy activity.

 Blue squares mean this is a medium level activity.

 Pink squares mean this is a more difficult activity. You'll have to think hard.

SORTING AND SETS

When your mom or dad says "clean your room!" they are really just trying to help you with your mathematics! When you clean up, you may group and order your toys so they can be found more easily. Each group of toys is called a **set**. Every toy is called an **element**.

THESE SHOES ARE MADE FOR WALKING

You can do this with a brother, sister, or friend.

1 How many shoes are there in the house? Ask an adult if you can collect them all together and put them in one big pile.

2 This is the set of all shoes in the house. Each shoe is an element of the set. How many shoes are there in the set? Let's hope it is an even number!

3 Find two colored towels. Sort the shoes into two sets on the towels: adult's shoes and children's shoes. Each of these groups is called a subset.

4 Can you sort them in any other way?

Dress shoes and everyday shoes.

Indoor and outdoor shoes.

Uncomfortable and comfortable shoes.

Left foot and right foot shoes.

Shoes that are smaller than your foot and shoes that are larger.

5 Sort them into sets that belong to each person in the house.

6 And last of all, can you sort them so that they go back to the right place in the house?

● To help you play these sorting games choose one shoe. Take turns to think of different words or phrases to describe the shoe.

● How many can you think of? Three... five... how about ten?

MORE IDEAS

● Try sorting out your pens and pencils into different groups.

● You could sort your pencils into those that need to be sharpened and those that are sharp. What other ways could they be sorted to help you find them more easily?

CARROLL DIAGRAMS

A set of elements have at least one thing, or **property**, in common. If you have a set of fruit you can say that any element in the set is either "an apple" or "not an apple." Carroll diagrams are a way of sorting information like this.

PICK 'N' MIX

Have you ever opened a large box of candy and then spent a long time looking for your favorite... or avoided the one with the chewy center that you hate! A Carroll diagram can help you to sort out the yummy from the yucky. First decide on something about the candy you really like... perhaps you like toffee... perhaps you hate chocolate.

1 In a Carroll diagram we call the headings **categories**. In this diagram toffee and chocolate will be the categories. Draw your diagram like the one at the top of page 9.

A candy that has toffee and chocolate would go here.

	Chocolate	Not chocolate
Toffee		
Not toffee		

One that has chocolate but no toffee would go here.

Where would you put a candy that has no chocolate and no toffee?

2 Sort out your candy. In which part of the diagram are your favorite candy? Where are your least favorite?

HELPFUL HINTS

● Most candy boxes give a guide to their contents on the side. Keep it handy. It might stop you from making a terrible mistake!

MORE IDEAS

● What else can you sort using Carroll diagrams? How about the laundry? (Ask an adult.)
● Try categories like "shirt" and "not shirt," and "adult" and "not adult."

VENN DIAGRAMS

The elements of a set don't always fall into two easy groups. An element might be a part of different sets at the same time. Venn diagrams are a useful way of showing this.

DOUBLE TROUBLE!
This is a game that uses a Venn diagram. Pick a subject for your set. What about animals?

1 Draw two overlapping circles as below, or make them from colored cardboard. Label each circle as a different subset.

Set
1pt.

3pts.

Subsets
2pts.

2 You might choose prehistoric and carnivorous animals. Each circle is a subset of the whole (universal) set of animals.

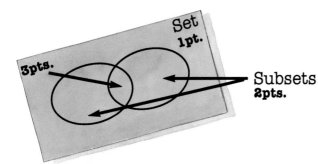

3 Think of any animal. Write it on a piece of cardboard and place it where it belongs on the diagram. A Stegosaur scores two points, a cow scores one point.

4 What about a carnivorous (meat-eating) animal? A lion scores two points.

5 If you can think of an animal that is carnivorous and prehistoric it would go in the striped intersection and score three points!

HELPFUL HINTS

● It might be useful to find books with animal facts and dinosaur facts to help you play this game.

MORE IDEAS

● You could make up your own game using other sets. How about the set of musical instruments. The two overlapping subsets could be electrical instruments and stringed instruments!

● Harder, but great fun, is to think up three overlapping sets. Try this one. How would you change the scoring system?

6 Have five turns each and see who can get the highest score.

Carnivorous animals

Animals with fur

Animals that live in water

THINKING LOGICALLY

When you woke up this morning you solved quite a tricky problem – getting dressed!

You had to **think logically**. What did you do first? What did you do next? Did you put your clothes on in the correct order and on the right parts of your body?!

THE SHOWMAN, HIS TIGER, A DUCK, AND THE SACK OF CORN

How good are you at thinking logically? This is an old problem. You need to help the showman cross a river with his tiger, duck, and sack of corn.

1 There is a boat but it is so small that it can only hold the showman and one of the others.

2 The showman can't leave the tiger with the duck as the duck will be eaten. He can't leave the duck with the corn for fear of losing all the corn. How does he get across?

3 Find some toys and pretend they are the showman, tiger, duck, and corn. Make a river with blue paper.

4 Put all the toys on one side of the river. What would happen if the showman took the tiger over first? Is it a better plan to take the corn? Would it be a good idea to take the duck?

HELPFUL HINTS

● Have you worked out the first thing that the showman should transport across the river?

● It couldn't be the tiger, because the duck would be left on its own with the tasty corn!

● He couldn't take the corn because the tiger would be all alone with the juicy duck!! So, the first thing that needs to go is the... duck.

● What happens next? One last clue: The showman can bring something back across the river with him if he needs to.

MORE IDEAS

● The Towers of Hanoi is an ancient logic problem. You need to move the pile of disks from the red square to the green square. Only one disk may be moved at a time. A larger disk can never be placed on a smaller disk. You could play this game with three coins of different sizes. What is the smallest number of moves it takes to do it?

5 When you think you have figured out how it could be done, make up a short story with the toys and tell it to your friends.

PLAY TO WIN!

Have you ever played Tic-tac-toe? Can anyone beat you? If you play cleverly, you can make sure that you never lose! To play this game well you need to use logic. There are many games that depend on skill and **strategy**. Chess and Checkers are good games; perhaps you could also find out about Othello or Go.

DIAMONDS

Diamonds is an ancient game of skill for two players that some believe was played by Arabian princes.

1 First you need to make a square board divided into 16 squares. Cut out 20 counters, you could make them diamond-shaped.

2 When you play Tic-tac-toe you need to get a line of three to win. But in Diamonds you lose if three diamonds are placed in a line. The line might be vertical, horizontal, diagonal, even if there is a gap in the line.

3 Each player has 10 diamonds. Take turns to place a diamond on a square.

You lose

14

● Before you put a diamond on the board look carefully! Check each row and don't forget the diagonal lines.

4 The winner takes all the diamonds on the board! Start the game again and play with your new set of diamonds. The game ends when one person has won all the diamonds.

MORE IDEAS

● What is the greatest number of diamonds you could fit on the board without getting three in a straight line? It is easy to place 6. Can you fit on any more?

● It is fun to try this game on a 64-square chessboard. You can play with up to six players!

THE RIGHT PLACE

Finding the right place to send, store, or find things can be a tricky business. Look at the address on some letters that have been sent to you. Your address might have a house number, street name, the town you live in, state, zip code, and perhaps country, – lots of information to make sure that the letter reaches the right person.

AMAZING MONSTER MOUNTAINS
Use colored cardboard, pens, and glue to make the monsters and mountain in the picture.

1 Are you brave enough to help them find their home on the mountain?

Here are some clues to help you.

● All the monsters on the right of the mountain have round, green bodies. The other monsters have red bodies.

● Monsters at the bottom of the mountain have short, green hair. All the other monsters have blue, curly hair.

● The monsters all have two eyes except the one at the peak that has three.

● All of the monsters on the mountain have triangular noses, two feet, and two arms.

3 Some of the places on the mountain are still empty. You might have to make some more monsters and put them in their homes.

HELPFUL HINTS

● When you are deciding where to put your monster check against all the clues one at a time. Then go through the clues and make a list of the different things you need to include in your drawing. Your list might look something like this:

green body
blue, curly hair
two eyes

MORE IDEAS

● You can make more great monster mountain puzzles with your friends. Draw a mountain, or trace the one on the page. Add more features like a cave or some trees.

● Next, make up some clues, then draw the monsters. Make sure they match the clues you have given!

DEFINITELY MAYBE

Do you think it will rain tomorrow? If you take a card from a deck what are the **chances** you will draw an ace? When mathematicians study questions like these they are studying the likelihood or probability of something happening.

FLIPPER

When you flip a coin into the air what might happen when it lands? Two things could happen. It might show a head or a tail. The likelihood of getting a tail is one chance in two, or you could say a half.

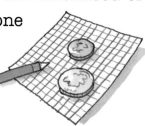

1 This is a game for three players. You need two different coins, a pencil, and some squared graph paper to keep score.

2 The first player gets a point if you can see two heads after the coins have been  flipped. The second player gets a point if you can see a head and a tail.

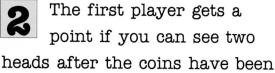

The third player gets a point if there are two tails.

3 Take turns to be the coin flipper and keep score of the points.

4 Flip the coins about 20 times each. Who is winning? Is this a fair game? Which team would you rather be if you started the game again?

HELPFUL HINTS

Coin 1   Coin 2

● It makes it easier to understand this game if you use two different coins when you are flipping. You can find out which team has the best chance of winning by looking at all the possible things that could happen – the possible outcomes. There are four possibilities:

● There is only one chance in four of getting two heads and only one chance in four of getting two tails, but there are two chances in four of getting one of each!

● What are you going to choose next time?

MORE IDEAS

● Try playing Flipper with four coins. Which would be the best "team" to choose? All heads? How about two heads and two tails? Do you think three tails and a head would be best? Experiment, find out, then challenge your friends to a game!

● Why is "heads I win, tails you lose" an unfair way to decide who wins when you flip a coin?

TAKE A CHANCE

There are many games that use a mixture of luck, skill, and strategy. Backgammon is an exciting game to play, so is Monopoly. Good players are those that know how to make the best decision whatever the throw of the die or draw of the cards. Can you work out the best way to play Sweaty palms?

SWEATY PALMS

1 You need some dried beans and three or more players for this game – in fact the more players you have the better! Each player secretly holds one or two beans in his or her hand.

2 Next, everyone tries to guess the total being held by the whole group. The person who makes the best guess is the winner!

3 How many beans do you think these four players are holding? Is 3 a good guess? Are some guesses better than others?

4 Play the game a few times. Do some numbers come up more often than others? What are your chances of making a correct guess?

HELPFUL HINTS

● Be careful when you make your guess.

● Remember that each player must hold one or two beans. If everyone is holding one what is the total being held? If everyone is holding two what is the total being held now?

MORE IDEAS

● To get really good at Sweaty palms look at all the different ways the numbers could be made in a game with four players. How many ways are there of making 4? What about 8? Can you figure out how many ways there are of making the other possible numbers; 5, 6, and 7?

● The number that can be made the most different ways is the best choice!

SPIN THE SPINNER

Many games of chance depend on the roll of a die or a spin of a disk. Can you think of some? When a die is rolled there are six possible **outcomes** – either a 1, 2, 3, 4, 5, or 6.

SIX-A-SIDE SOCCER SPIN

1 Have you ever played five-a-side soccer? This is a game of six-a-side with spinners! You need to make one spinner for every person playing. You will need cardboard, scissors, and some pens or pencils. Each player must choose a team from the grid below.

2 Pick a team from the grid below. Each team has its own numbers.

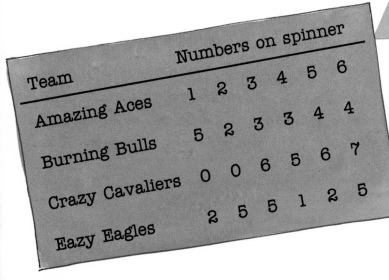

Team	Numbers on spinner					
	1	2	3	4	5	6
Amazing Aces	5	2	3	3	4	4
Burning Bulls	0	0	6	5	6	7
Crazy Cavaliers	2	5	5	1	2	5
Eazy Eagles						

3 Cut the cardboard into a six-sided regular hexagon like this. Draw and decorate your team's spinner with the numbers and colors and push a sharp pencil through the center.

4 To play a match against another team, spin the spinner. The spinner that comes to rest on the highest number wins the match.

5 If your team is the Cavaliers and four of you are playing then you might keep a scorecard like this:

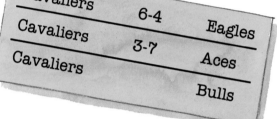

Cavaliers		Eagles
	6-4	
Cavaliers		Aces
	3-7	
Cavaliers		Bulls

HELPFUL HINTS

● You can find out which teams are the best by working out all the possible outcomes when two of the spinners are spun. You could make a color chart to compare the Cavaliers and the Aces:

	1	2	3	4	5	6
7	C	C	C	C	C	C
6	C	C	C	C	C	D
5	C	C	C	C	D	A
6	C	C	C	C	C	D
0	A	A	A	A	A	A
0	A	A	A	A	A	A

Cavaliers (vertical axis) / **Aces** (horizontal axis)

● There are 36 possible outcomes. There are **20 possibilities** that the Cavaliers could win (red), 3 of a draw (yellow), and 13 for the Aces to win (blue). So, the Cavaliers have a better team.

6 Play ten matches against each team. Don't count the draws. Which team did you choose? Why did you think it had the best chance of winning? If you played again, would you choose the same team?

GRAPHS AND CHARTS

Graphs and charts are used by mathematicians to make information clearer or make certain facts stand out. If you were collecting information to find your friends' favorite cartoon character you might begin by keeping a tick list. But you can show this information more clearly in a bar graph.

THE TOP TEN CHART

You could use a bar graph to help plan the music for a party. You would need to find out the type of music that everyone would want to dance to. What information do you need to help you decide? What are your friends' favorite pop stars? First, draw out a tally table like the one on the left.

1 Now ask your friends to name three pop stars they like. Write down each name mentioned and put a check by it each time that name gets a vote.

12
11
10
9
8
7
6
5
4
3
2
1

Pop Star
A

Pop St
B

2 Next, draw out a bar graph using the information you collected in your tick list. Each pop star gets one colored square for each vote. You can use your graph to find out which pop music is favorite!

HELPFUL HINTS

● You might find it easier to use graph paper when you are filling in your bar graph. Make sure the paper is long enough to fit in the pop star with the most checks. If you don't plan carefully you might run out of room at the top of the graph!

Pop Star
C

Pop Star
D

Pop Star
E

MORE IDEAS

● Another graph like a bar graph is a pictogram. Instead of coloring in a block, draw a small picture of each item that gets a vote. You could use a pictogram to plan the food at your party. Collect information about what everyone likes to eat and try to chart the information in a pictogram.

DATASTREAMS

Some information gathered in experiments is continuous! When you are young your growth is continuous – it doesn't stop. If you measured your height every year you could make a graph of the data. It may look like there are sudden big jumps in the graph but in fact you did grow continuously over the year.

UPS AND DOWNS

Have you ever taken part in an important event like a school play? Throughout the day you might sometimes feel happy and at other times sad. A datastream is a good way of showing this.

1 Look at this graph. It shows the feelings of someone taking part in a school play, from when she wakes up in the morning to when the performance finishes.

2 The graph has been written on (or annotated) to describe why she felt happy or sad at different times.

Wake up and remember play

Happy

Go to school

Sad

Eat horrible lunch

8.00

10.00

12.00

2.00

4.00

Finish work before play

3 Choose your own special event and draw out a graph like this one.

Prepare costume for play

Play starts

Audience claps

Forget my lines

4 Next, annotate the graph to help describe why you felt either happy or sad at different times in the day.

0

8.00

HELPFUL HINTS

● You could start the graph by drawing a horizontal line across the page.

● Mark a point on the left and, next to it, the time you woke up. Now draw a vertical line straight up.

● Write in the time on the horizontal line. You might find it easier  to think about how you felt at the time you woke up, then mark a point; how you felt when you got to school, then mark a point. Mark points throughout the day and finally join up the points to make a curve.

MORE IDEAS

● Sometimes when you take part in an exciting event you might not feel just happy or sad. You could feel a mixture of both feelings – at the end of the play you could feel happy that everyone thought you had done well, but sad that the play had finished. How could you show that on the graph?

A PIECE OF PIE!

Many types of graphs and charts are used to show information clearly. Pie charts are usually circle shaped. They are used to show fractions of a whole. Why do you think it is called a pie chart? This pie chart shows how children traveled to their school. Which part of the pie is the largest? It is easy to see that most children walked to school.

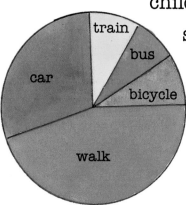

WHAT DID YOU DO TODAY?
Did you know that your mom and dad spend a lot of their time lying around doing nothing! You can prove it with a pie chart! You will need some lined paper, pens, ruler, adhesive tape, and some scissors.

1 First you need to gather some information. Ask your mom or dad how much time everyday they spend on eating, the amount of time at work, time spent watching T.V., the amount of time traveling, and the amount of time sleeping.

2 Next, cut out a long bar from the lined paper about 5 inches wide stretching over 24 lines. Each line represents one hour of the day.

3 If two hours are spent traveling, color in two bars. Use a different color for each activity. When you have filled in the 24 bars loop the strip over into a circle and stick the ends together. Rest the circle on

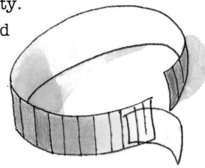

some paper, draw around it, and mark off the points for each activity. Draw a line from the points to the center and color in the different sections.

HELPFUL HINTS

● When you are collecting your information the time doesn't need to be exact. Measurements to the nearest hour or half hour will do.

MORE IDEAS

● You can use pie charts to find the amount of time a T.V. channel gives to different types of programs. Look at a T.V. guide and choose a channel. How much time is given to news, cartoons, movies, or other categories? Turn the information into a pie chart.

COMMON GRAPHS

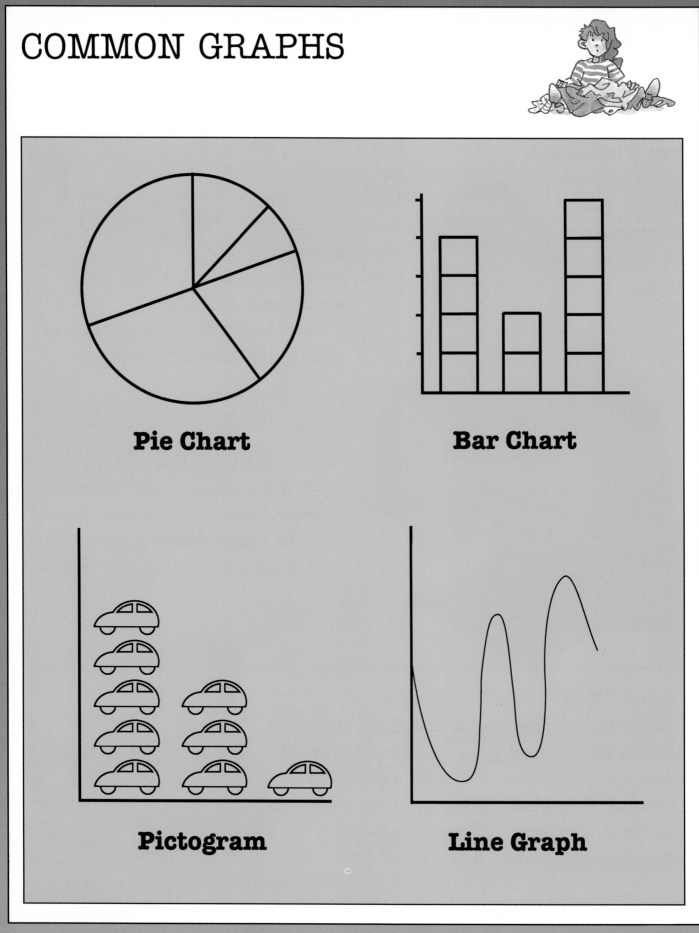

Pie Chart

Bar Chart

Pictogram

Line Graph

GLOSSARY

Category
If you were sorting animals into sets, first you would have to decide on the categories you wanted to use. One category could be animals that eat meat, so a lion and a dog would both belong to this category.

Chance
It depends on chance whether you throw the number you want on a die. Sometimes you can work out your chances – if you flip a coin, you have one chance in two that it will show a head.

Element
Each item that is in a set is called an element, so in a set of shoes, one shoe is an element of that set.

Graph
A graph is a way of showing information so that it is quick and easy to understand and use. Pie charts, bar graphs, pictograms, and line graphs are all different types of graphs.

Outcome
An outcome is what happens as a result of other things happening first.

Possibility
A possibility is something that might happen. When you throw a die, there are six possibilities. You might throw a 1, 2, 3, 4, 5, or a 6. Throwing a 7 is not a possibility because there is no 7 on a die.

Property
Items in a set all have properties or things that can describe them. One property of an apple is that it is a fruit. Another property is that it has a round shape. An apple can belong to a set of apples, or a set of things with a round shape, or to a set of fruit.

Set
When mathematicians put things into groups, each group is called a set. All the things in the set have something the same about them.

Strategy
A strategy is another word for a plan. You need a good strategy to outwit your opponent and win games like Checkers.

Thinking logically
If you can think logically, you can use facts and careful reasoning to solve problems.

INDEX

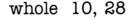